Gold

Naomi B.

Gold

Olympia Publishers
London

www.olympiapublishers.com
OLYMPIA PAPERBACK EDITION

A CIP catalogue record for this title is
available from the British Library.

ISBN: 978-1-80074-545-2

This is a work of fiction.
Names, characters, places and incidents originate from the writer's
imagination. Any resemblance to actual persons, living or dead, is
purely coincidental.

First Published in 2022

Olympia Publishers
Tallis House
2 Tallis Street
London
EC4Y 0AB

Printed in Great Britain

Dedication

To the ones who planted the seed I was
And who made me grow
Into a wise oak tree—

To my sisters—
To all my sisters—

To Inès,
My very first reader
And the best, most loyal
Friend
A joyful, hopeful, destroyed
Heart
Can wish for—

And to Gold
The breath of my first piece
The sister of my shell and core—

Acknowledgements

Thank you Maman et Papa. Thank you for building the path I'm now walking on. Without you I wouldn't have the heart I have, the hope I have, the determination and the courage I have and often remind myself to use. Thank you for everything you have given and taught me. Thank you for your love and infinite patience.

Thank you, my sweet little sisters, Kenza and Maïlys. You are my joy, my mirrors, my twins, the loves of my life. I am only one third of myself when you are not around.

Thank you Papy et Mamie. Thank you for teaching me youth, life and joy. Thank you for your incredible support, energy, generosity, infinite love and patience. You are the ones I see when I hear about true love. You are the bright colours of my childhood, my best childhood memories. Thank you forever.

Thank you Inès, my closest friend, first reader and supporter. Thank you for listening to me so very patiently, for reading my pieces five times at least, for giving me your advice, your precious opinion. Thank you for being such a loyal friend.

Thank you, Gold. You have been my first true love, the first I risked it all for. I have loved you like a pagan worships the sun. My heart will always be coloured with the colour of your skin. I regret nothing.

Thank you, my former teachers and professors. You have taught me to read, write and think above the mountains I could see. You have seen something in me and encouraged me to go as far as I could, or even farther.

Thank you, all the bright authors of my world. Thank you for taking my five-year-old hand and since then leading me to a secret, imaginary and perfect world I have always craved for. Thank you for teaching me empathy, love, determination, respect and passion. Thank you for putting words on my often-inexpressible emotions.

Thank you, women. Thank you for inspiring me, for being so strong, for teaching me. Thank you for making me feel part of the strongest, most glowing group of creatures on Earth.

Thank you, Olympia Publishers, for making my dream come true. For helping me make my voice heard.

Thank you everyone who has encouraged and supported me. Thank you for your support and enthusiasm.

Illustrator of front cover – **Louis Plunian**

SOIL

My voice is an instrument
That hasn't been practised—
I'm a lost guitar
An out-of-tune piano—

If I could utter a sound
Would it be a note
          —or a shout?

I am

unfit

inadequate

HANDICAPPED—

My mouth is a world of silence.

I wonder why
We wanted to grow up so fast—
When all we want now
Is to find a way back—

Everything ends
And it's a giant's breath
That ices my chest
And mine
Is frozen
When I count the years—

That visualized countdown—
A clock in my head—

I'm in love with life so much
Its changing colours and emotions
That I'll wait for the very last strike of the bell
To go to bed—

I have created
This secret room
At the back of my head—
I lie down in it—
Play hide and seek—
It's sometimes dark, cold and lonely
But at least I know it
It's like family—
It's a protective world
A selfish spot
Where I can grow roses—or disappear—

It would be a second birth
To get out then in—
I need to be born
Again—

I'm a dark, dark lady
Something tore me inside—a long time ago—

And there are times when—
Pain
Is a knife
Dropping poison
In my waters and blood—

Times when—
I turn the clock back
And she rises—whispers
She never left—

And she bites
Where it already hurts
Builds her castle
Again
Arranges her empire
Reborn from sand—

And—almighty—
Her river wakes up suddenly
And it's an angry ocean in me
—enraged waves—
Then I bite my lower lip from the inside
And—vampire—
She crawls up to my throat
To get a taste
Of my sorrow.

She has all the answers—
She once told me—
Emptiness is all it takes
To make me happy—
I am the strongest
In all the versions
You'll ever be—
I saved us:
Starvation
Was the only option
To stay alive—
Don't you remember
Feeding your mouth was
Feeding *her*
That gut and heart fed-on monster—
I made us stronger
Tougher
I rose a rage
And the remaining weight
Is a left-over—
The price
I'll make you pay.

Eyes on Time
Past and future—
I fear I might use my view too much
And forget the core—
The movements—

The tap
of emotions
is locked—

If I
turn it back on
a rush—

Will flood the room.

Pain has the skin of a crocodile
The weight of an elephant
And loneliness the slip of the lizard
That knows the way to my guts—by heart
That lurks and slithers
Before attacking—my heart—

Another black dot
One can see in the memories of the dead
Or in paintings and photographs—
Dressed in petticoats and dark well-fastened silk
Standing on shores—

Her Will—hidden behind the cloth of her dress
Corseted—gasping for air—
Her Passion—floundering like a trapped wild eel
In her own flesh—and head—
The tumult in her soul—one could catch in her eye
If willing to explore—
Shows in the complexity of her twisted locks of
long, brown hair—

Dressed in petticoats and dark well-fastened silk
Eyes lost on distant, invisible seas—
I suppose those black dots will remain
Black dots—for centuries—

Melancholy is a snake
That seems to be smitten with me—
It comes back now and then
Can' t get enough of me—

It settles in my brain—and unpacks
Let' s a puff of grey mist inside my head
And sings a poisoned
Lullaby to my limbs—

Still and mute—

I drop my arms—

Lose the fight—

Swallowed

Digested

By
        slithering
                    melancholy.

Red wild woman
Who are you?
I wish I could let you
Out—
My skin is iron
And you knock so hard—

While my hair is tidy
And well arranged
In a bun—sign of control—
Yours is fury, frizzy and free
Wild as fire—

And I can see you
Glimpsing in the mirror—

It frightens the girl in me—

But if you give in
My heart will stop
And emotions will be—memories—
And I'll be decisions—and principles—only.

Two languages
Two continents
Two
Different attractions

Too passionate
Emotional
Too sensible
Too proud and free

Too hot
Too cold
Two colours

Two
Women
In me—

My face is a graveyard
Of still-born emotions—

There's an echo—in my head
Like the drums in a melody
There's a voice—calling my name
Begging to break free.

She knows no word
Only screams—
Her tongue's a whip
Spits lava spit—

She burns my mouth
And gallops wild—oh how wild—

Heart-washed
I feel
Heart-washed

Cause she said
To let go
Of this lawless, savage, loose monster
Who hides in me—
Undergroundly—
Who whispers, possesses, bewitches me—

But what if
She's too much to handle
What if
She's uncontrollable—

What if she breaks me and all
The life I know

I know what Want feels like—
The impression of
Living with
An empty glass inside
Waiting to be filled—

I miss the language of my
Ancestors
Its rhythm on the lips
Its curls on the tongue—

This is why
I've been in search for
Words
All along—

When I'm dead, she said
Think of me at rest
Freed from all my thoughts at chest—

Selfish I'm allowed to be now
And sad as well
About a life I'll have to part with
A life I haven't completed
With dreams
I'll never make real—

Sometimes I notice
A cheap painting on a wall
Or an ugly cardigan hanging on a chair.
And I think
I'll miss that—and I'll miss that—
And even that—old people's skins and the taste of
milk—
And suddenly I imagine
What the world will be like
When I have left it
And I find it tiring to feel
What won't be felt by me
The nothingness—and the emptiness—
How can I guess what others will see?

But then I rejoice in remembering
Things will always be
What they've always been.
And you will smile, darling
And keep on living.

Walking in the dark
Naked
Her arms along her ribs
The child could not see a thing—

And when she lifted an arm
An invisible reprimand
Tapped her hand—
And forced it back down—

Uncle—
You come back now and then
When hearts hustle—

You are a shadow—

A portrait hanging
In the air
We grew up in.

This little girl you see
Walking timidly
Who step after step
Leans under the weight
Of all the questions and self-discipline
She put on her own shoulders
At the age of four—

This little girl you see
Who confined you for twenty years
Starved you of love and
Made life a mystery—

This little girl you see
Reach out your hands
And put them delicately
On her sweet child neck
And squeeze very hard
Till she can't call for help—
You'll see blue veins on her peachy skin
Make sure they explode make sure
Till her eyes don't come out
Don't let her go—

This little girl you see
Suck her dear life out
And become the red wild woman
That she couldn't be.

In an unknown and secret land
A child was born
She still has her lids closed—
Don't open them too soon
The fairy said
Relish this moment
Of ignorance
Of innocence
You will never find again.

After peeling—shred after shred
Of my skin
She spreads my ribs
With her fingernails
And lets me lay there
Pumping blood—chest cavity naked—
And she scratches all the question marks on her way
To the bleeding—beating—frightening truth—

When she is done
Will it be gold that she sees—
Or some expired stone
Worthless to be dug out?

therapy.

Control over oneself is the result of experience.
A long, long lesson
To a young child taught.
Can be used as a shield—or a sword.

Then you can be a knight
From the royal—Chivalry
Be the best soldier
Kill hundreds from your distant, fortified

HIDEAWAY

But then
Chivalry deserts—
And no more sense—no more meaning
It is a frightening—*feeling*
Of *tempting liberty*
A big hole gripping your foot
And then you're done
With Chivalry.

All those roads in my brain
Leading to my heart—
I wish I knew the way
To the secrets—of me being a secret—
I wish I could read Braille—

I want my mind to be on holiday
On holiday

                                        In a big, empty house

                         Somewhere
                     in Canada or Italy—

        I want my mind to be on holiday

                         On a

                         Quiet
                         Lonely

                     Holiday—

40

I am the ocean
I am like her waters
elusive and tangible—

I have a secret
hidden behind composure
and docility—

Soothing and cruel
I dance and make
the waves waltz
deep—

                    I recognize the ocean's music
                              —in my head
                                whirling—
                         dizzying—sound
                          blinding me—

My hair is wild—
Legacy of an unknown world—
My mother used to pull it—tame it—
Tie it—in a pretty fastened bun
At the top of my six-year-old head—

I wish it had known more wind
More tornadoes—possibly sin—

Self-discipline:
Don't you dare think it over
Don't you dare change your mind
Don't you dare back out
Weak mind—

Like a boomerang it flew back
And hit me in the face—
Monster, I shouted
You cloud of poisonous rain—

You keep coming back, don't you
Flooding me with anxiety
Are you so hungry that you
Can't live without the sugar in me—

Oh, the fight won't be a school trip but
I'll be the monster, you'll see
I'll scorch your heart and make you bleed
Cause it's either *you* or *me.*

I was about to settle
In a cosy boring life
A regular one
A tight little one
A comfortable lie

When suddenly my conscience
Held—me back
And screaming, shouting—dancing in the night
Stopped me half way
And gave birth to a mess
That I called confusion first
But that I'll call *me* instead—

Is it okay to call myself
A *girl*—most of the time—
And not
A *woman*—
It's just that it feels like
Being a woman
Demands—requires—so much
Energy
Strength
Certainties and
Confidence—

I'm still learning
—I'm an apprentice in
Womanhood.

GROW

I'll be free
When I can climb up pine trees.

It is—
A scream in my head
A confusion
An explosion
A little chaos
Of little thoughts
And of questions—

I'm far from being religious
I turn my eye away from sacraments
And biblical stories sound like fairy tales to me—
Yet I cannot help but wonder at
Feel conventional respect for
The profound sound
Of long white or dark gowns
On a cobbled cathedral floor—

I for a long time thought
Boys were different
From us
That their hearts were
Less profound—

What a shock to realize
That they can cry too
That the taste of their tears is as salty
As ours—

The storm explosion
And the rush of the rain
Echo
    The rage in my heart
                        The letting go—

.

Sometimes I wash my hair
Hoping
The steam of the water
Will wash
The steam in my head
Away—

When your old friends
Have drowned in their lives already—

And you

Have only

Moistened a toe—

Empty insides
Balloon head
So, light you feel so light—

Girl—you've been told ugly lies
Your body is power
Your tool, your child—

Trust me, I'm your sister
I knew hunger for years
I still remember
The creasings of my stomach
When fasting made me—hangover—for quiet, long
hours—

Girl—I know your rage—
A fourteen-year-old anger is an army of Undead—

Girl—you'll be the strongest
Among the strongest—
You'll be a woman.

How I hate it when they
Think curves
And not
Tears—
Skin
And not brains—

How they use their hands when
We want their ears
How they
Are children
When at twelve we learned
That we were
Women.

Three
Siamese
Three
magnets
undistinguishable—
misses

Three
vases
of different shapes
but the same
water
was poured in—

I'm amputated when the world
gets in the way—
When the language we speak
is blurred
by the miles—
the far away.

Don't look down on
Children who play
Till night in the street.

It's
a carcass
that
I'll
carry
at the
end
of my
journey—
My bones
will
have
known
change
and my
flesh—
pain.

been.
ever
have

would

it

than

stronger
be
will
body
My

again—

walk
and
up

stand
to

learned
and
grown
have
will
I

My books are the friends
I bring with me when I travel.
They remind me home
Is anywhere I choose to be.

How many thoughts
Have you heard—
How much distress
Have you witnessed—
How many hearts
Have you relieved—

Over the years—

Woods—

Thoughts
are leprechauns
—they
jump
and travel
—they
never
stay in place—they
climb hills
bounce
—they
wear you down—

Thoughts
dance—
like
apprentice ballerinas—they
attempt
at perfection
—they
never reach it—they
crash
break their ankles
—they
keep flying—

A garden beneath my skin—a path
An inky trace of dark marks—

I gave my limb as an offering
Placed power into her hands
—it felt like the most natural thing to trust a
perfect stranger—

Then the needle teased my skin
Attempting at penetration
Vibrations—a tickling
Then numbness
A thin sucking
—a vicious devouring and
licking
of the dripping drops—

The blood oozing along my arm
Unexpectedly
Flushed my cheeks—

Hurt me all you want
I can feel my soul rising—

I will

alwaysalwaysalwaysalwaysalwaysalwaysalways

be on women's side.

You reproach us for the trees
Whose seeds you planted
For the waterfalls
You poured water in
For the buildings
You architected.

I used to hate
my frizzy hair—
Wish for
straight
silky
wings
out of my head—

But now I see
my grandmother
and her sisters
and their
mother
and their
—untold— stories
in the
rebellions
of my curls.

Songs

of the

desert

dance

on my

skin.

I wear her face on mine
Her twin, they say—
But I'm her free version
The enraged—lucky—rude
Shout
My grandmother never let out—

She had hands as
Thick
As the dough
She'd tame
On Friday afternoons—

Sometimes
Her fingers would get lost
In my hair
When she braided it
—like a spell—
And it squeaked!

But I'd feel the knowledge
A *bond*
In the circles her nails would make

As her hair was mine
And belonged
To a past—we *shared*—
Of long, dark flames—

Now she is no more
And the plaits on my head
Have long been untied—

She entered the land of memories
And we look up—standing
Where she'll ever remain
Hair squeakings
Broad smiles

And a laugh like
Sparkles.

She counted on her fingers
Who was left:
One, two, three are gone
And childhood
With them—

She thought—
Siblings who leave
Are the burden of old age.

The need to feel something
To wake what sometimes doesn't feel mine
To give birth to my own body
To shake awake this flesh
That has been so sleepy—

I need to starve myself
I need to exhaust myself
I want to
Walk walk walk
Climb climb climb
Till I fall down on my knees
Till I beg for water
Till I pray for breeze—

Bless the person who invented ink.
They must have known
How heavy
Thoughts
Can be.

I have no idea where I am
But I'm not really worried—at the moment
There's the sound of the water
Dripping over drops
And the eye of a little duck—on me—
I'm not really worried
There's the silence of standing reeds
And the glistening of the Stockholm Sea
Reflecting history and natural
Peace—
There's cold wind—running in my hair
And a blue winter sky—over me
So why would I worry
About having no idea where I am—

At the shore
Of the calm winter Stockholm Sea
I—eventually—
Breathe—and accept the idea
To let all those black dots in my head
Turn into wild northern fish
Diving into and getting lost
In the calm winter Stockholm sea—

I'm a traveller
I'm a hiker
Walker—
I'm a tiny moving
Piece of flesh
And I swallow the wind—

When I look at trees
I remember where Truth is—

The sea doesn't share her secrets—
That's why she keeps
Her darkest blue
Out of reach—

Spices, smells, colours—light, summer, flavours—

Want in me
For a part of my body
The ignorance of a past the importance of blood
Those curved letters—and those oriental
mysteries—

The language the rhythm the children the colour of
the saffron—

The smoothness of the honey the thickness of the
oil
Women's hands digging—
Those words those sayings those—curious—prayers—

The pain of not being whole this hollow in my
stomach this emptiness—insatiable
Like the loss of a twin—
This need this call
From myself to myself
This look behind for a step forward—

                                This music
                        That enters my heart
                           And lays on my hips
                          For a natural dance
                         The dance of a memory
                             Far in the blood

                      The song of grandmothers
                               Of superstitions
                      The awakening of ancestors

Calling—

And
This comfortable certainty to be able to be
Everywhere
To know
Everything
To be a traveller—

Even though my face is a question
For the eyes
Even though my skin is an enigma
In their eyes
I have the memory of travelling—wombs
The memory of hearts—in love.

My mother used to dress up as
Wonder Woman
When she was five—

She kept her costume on
Raising us.

In the mirror it's you I see—
The blood I lose every month is
Yours—

Now I realize
The reason why
I've been so hurt
Is because I love you
So very much—
And the reason why
I pushed you out
Is because we are
So much alike—

They ask me where I'm from
What language I speak
Who I am—
I am unsure—
I belong to
No box
I wander—
Like a fish between waters
That wouldn't follow any flow.

I am *mixed-race*—
I am a bridge, a link—
I have the blood of
The oppressors the oppressed
The familiar customs
Of a foreign world
The foreign customs
Of a familiar world—

They say I am
Peninsular
The two almonds of my face
Carry the mystery—
My uncontrolled hair
In abundance
Of matted curls
—like a mess that doesn't know where to go—
My sunny skin that never gets red—
No one knows where I'm from—
I'm a fish between waters
That doesn't follow any flow.

Thresholds are sometimes
Borders.

Sometimes it feels
like the travellers in my womb
urge me
to cross the desert they were born in
and left.

They're still there—
The ones I thought were gone
The ones whose necks were bent under the weight of
snow—
That when blinded had hidden from the light
And had forgotten the taste of
Children's strokes
In summertime.
They're still there
Those dark roses
Shy with their intense red
They're rising—and beholding—
The sun.

STRETCH

A guardian angel, a fairy
Leant over my infant bed
And pronounced the magical recipe—

A touch of wisdom
An inch of sense
An infinite love for
Stories
A want for knowledge
A strong back
To carry books around
And the weight of disillusions
A daily attempt at courage
And above all
Sensitivity—
I can't do much against
Future sufferings
But I'll give you
The capacity to learn
The stubbornness to survive
To see the beauty
To finally understand
Love
Is all it takes to
Live.

The sun has arisen
Its light—an old friend
An entry—a come back
A long awaited—reunion—

I had heard its promise in the winter
But the greyness, darkness, monotony
Of those dying days
Made me doubt its very word—

Now I repent and rejoice
In the ever-resurrecting hope coming with it—hand
in hand
Ignoring the whisper
Reminding that Summer
Is mortal
—and has an end.

Every time I walk in my hometown

                    Disfiguring it with my footsteps

It is a love letter all around

                    That I softly scribe in its cement.

I'm a digger—

Surfaces don't interest me

I want to see the core—

                    The Heart beating—

Tired of—tiptoeing—whispering
She
Finally—brutally—desperately
Screams
Her rage to the wind.

What if we changed our view—
What if we saw that *she* is the one who
Englobes
Instead of welcomes—who
Wraps
Instead of receives—
She is after all the one who
Gives her scent to the sheets—

The two sides of my family
Have relied on different books—
So why do I feel betrayed
When I open any of them?

I read passages that attack
My femininity
By attacking
Other women

And I am all women—

And when they silent their voices
It is I too
Who want to shriek—

Under a great hat
A pale face
With strawberry lips—

She took a puff of a
Long, ancient
Cigarette
Then she exhaled—

Her confidence—

In her I saw
All women.

Daughter—
Your name will be
LIBERTY
I'll offer you
The bloody life
The beating one
The frightening one
That you'll look in the eye
And I'll be judged
For letting you free
The words I heard
You will not hear them
The gestures I didn't have
You will have them
I won't lie to you with
The rules I received
You will not be
Conditioned
You'll know how to love
Your choices will be yours
You'll be allowed to make mistakes
And I make the wish
You'll make many of them
You won't know where to go
And you'll survive a thousand Melancholies
You'll love until it disfigures
Your heart
You'll give yourself if you want to Give yourself
You'll be the slave of your passions Only
You'll have the fire of
Love
The vein of the open
Mind
And a generous
Heart
You'll scream your hate

You will be rude
Have a wet eye
And you'll follow your stomach
That crook we forget
The place of want
You will come

For love, for life
You will fall
Several times
And you'll come back to yourself
You won't be a pearl
A perfect woman
You will choose to be
A mistress
A spouse
A child
A mother
A storm
You'll be the flesh of my insanity
The scream of my scream
The removal of my fear
The killer of prejudices
The choice of choices
You will be free
Daughter
You will be.

Hometown walk:

How I love
Favours done
Hands holding
Shared snacks
Offered smiles
Strong-willed little girls—

Or when young people
Help old people
Carry half
Their weight
And cross the street—

How we thank with the tone
Of a *humane* heart—

Or how women walk with
Confidence
In the street—

How I love us sometimes.

Isn't it a wonder
That what we feel doesn't show
Even when it breaks in our stomachs—

I imagine clouds of
Flying—drifting—overwhelming
Emotions
That would overpopulate
Our space—

I was taught
The world is a dangerous place to live in
Girls are feasts
For starving ravens—

But what about
My hunger

Freedom

The wave—the anguish

The thoroughbred   —   racing   —
                 in me   —

Let me run wild as a free spirit
Let me walk miles, curse and risk it—

Grandparents:
The secret
Delicacies
They've been offering each other
For half a century—
Like unspoken gifts
Thrown in the air
To make the other's life sweeter
Than caramel—

Like ancient princesses
She crossed a sea to find
A man she barely knew—

She brought her lovely heart
And gave second chances
Then fifty stars she drew—

—meeting point

I have

come to

see the

              SpArK1E

when

two cultures

meet

           in one person.

If I hook silver in *my ears*
If I paint *my nails* red
If I spend minutes drawing a black line on *my eyelids*—
It is not because I'm vain—

It is because I know
I deserve
To decorate *myself.*

You
Have not known
Submission
You
Have not known
Shame

You
Have not known
Muzzling
You
Have not known
Fear

You
Shall not know
Rage

You
Shall never know
Sisterhood.

—blessing

Bisexuality
is a superpower.

Two possibilities—
Duality—
Two cravings—
In one body.
A murdered restriction
To fall in love—
An opportunity
To see beauty.

I'm a curious being—
Curiosity
Is being able to see
Human beings.

Flawless
Bodies
Are like
Pages
With no
Stories.

Give me truth—blank and bare
Give me unpolished honesty—
Give me facts—straight and fair
But please don't ever lie to me.

I'd rather bleed from a well-cut wound
Than smile for the false hope you give me—
I'd rather die a little or mourn
Than torment over hypocrisy.

Sue me:
Pride and stubbornness
Came from my mother to me.

Free the hounds
Free the dragon in my soul—

Free them all—

There is beauty—and strength—in sin
In unclean souls and suffering—
I won't be the one who'll judge their neighbour's
worst stumbling—
I'll be the one who
Smiles at them and offers their hand
When the rest of the world
Whispers their name—

As there isn't one drop of perfection in my sweat
And I am glad my heart is made
Of distress and jealousy
Of roars, shrieks and angry poundings—

For sin is found
In the wild of my soul
And I'll climb hills and mountains to catch it
For sin is life
And I will not pray
Or apologize
For reaching out—

I am not take-away meat
I am not a dish you can help yourself with—
I am the five-star restaurant
You'll never get in.

Boldness
Hope
Purity—
Purity—of hope—and boldness—
Are lent with youth.

I'm tired of tiptoeing—
Next time I'll rush *ungracefully* with my impatience
Won't try to mute
My noisy, rapid footsteps' rambling.

I'm tired of apologizing—
Next time I'll curse—and roar—
And won't say sorry.

I'm tired of smiling—
Cause I'm always in a rush
Or overthinking
And I won't care a straw
If you don't find me jolly enough
To call me pretty.

Next time I'll show up
With my scars, my inner injuries
Half attentive—cause my head will be
In the clouds
Between her legs
Or in a Brontë story.

—oh how proud I can be—how cold—
—how burning cold—
—how stoic and mute—

But a rabid, wild whirl—
A heart racing like a thoroughbred's—

In Italy
I met the beauty of the world—
I met love
Its shape, colour—
I met history—
I met the sun
And the desire to linger
And live
        Finally—

I tripped and fell down
Struggled to
Stand back up—
The lift doors wouldn't open for me—

But I saw
Distinctively
With the eyes of the
Unlucky—who
Never really stood—
And I shivered—
And my *cold judgement*
Melted in the warmth
Of their humanity—
And I felt
The equilibrium—of peace—
The peace of humility.

I'm a summer girl—

In summer I embrace the world
Enter the breeze like a new element
That has been asleep the rest of the year
And finally hears the sun's calling—

I'm the leaf joyfully dancing
In the morning air—
I'm the sweet taste
Of your juicy peach—
I'm the cat resting
In the shade—
I'm the tanned skin
Of the underdressed—
I'm the burning air
You can't escape from—
I'm the heat—the passion—the sweat—

I am the sun's servant—

And I'm jealous of it
For it gets to light up your shoulders
And turn your eyes into liquid honey
When I'm not there—

I fell in love with summer—

But summer never lingers
And I always fall for those
Who never stay—

Like draughts—they follow their call
And I
Wait for the next ray—

The body is
A heart and
A sex.
Nothing else.
They are the core—the temple—of
Vulnerability—
Of misery and
Mountains.

I don't need languid eyes—

I want someone able to
Hold my heart in their hands
And—
Undisgusted—
In love with the blood dripping from it
In thick, dark tears—
Kiss
The beating organ
Raw—

A new truth—

Reflection is all good
It's a comfort—a pillow
It's a path of
Safety
Of fewer mistakes and stumblings.

But it doesn't have what Instant has
Truth
Meaning
The sensation of—living.

It sometimes takes time
·   To accept
Short-life passions have
Beauty—and authenticity—
In them.
Their shorter truth is no less dizzying
Than a life of Reason—

My ribcage has opened up—
I'll never look down again.

I was waiting for someone to
Reach out
Listen
And tell me
I'm allowed.

She found it in the
woods
somehow
my voice—

It was a
silver ball
hidden
under countless piles of oak tree leaves—

And
careful not to make me
drunk
with it
she
gave it back to me
key after key

With
spells
I'd never heard of

made of
asking and
listening and
tearing—

Now I remember:
I remember
what it feels like to
       sing—

There are souls
Whose exquisite delicacy reaches my heart
—my tumbling heart—
Each time
Shaken—

Then the cloths of those adored souls
Seem to dance all wild
Tease
And twist
Around my steaming heart.

SUN

gold

I have this bliss in me
That could make me shed tears
Of love for your sorrow.

In the middle of the crowd
You laugh so loud—
Internal pains forgotten—

Excessive in smiling
You offer your lights
While—already given—
I keep looking at you.

I am the hidden one
The invisible one
Deaf to my frightened Reason
Since I bathe in your warmth in wintertime
And I let myself sink—

Or from a small, gloomy room
You let me gaze at you.

I am the contemplative
Of your efforts—
I am the spectator
Of your movements—
Your Observatory—
Your wide Audience—
I am the one
Who eyes you in silence.

Every day without seeing you is

Time

Poured in emptiness.

shelovesmeshelovesmenotshelovesmeshelovesmenotshelovesmeshelovesmenotshelovesme

When I don't see her
On the dreadful, painful
Five days of the week
I almost forget
How beautiful she is—

And then I meet her
On the long awaited
    HOLY DAYS
And I'm crushed—
Broken—
I can't breathe—
My heart pounds—
My muscles tighten
At the extreme—

And it's a physical pain
And astonishment
To see how
Magnificent
Her light is—

My eyes stop on women's backs

                              Admiring of the beauty

        The stability and extreme elegance—

                    But it is on yours that they stay
                    And that my hands want to lay.

We are not a triangle—
We are a line
For he looks at me
While I stare at you
And you—stare at me too.

I close my eyes and there I go—
I slide down the hills of your ankles
And cross the soft path
Where my hands become as light as birds—
I slow down for the delicious ascent
Where the silk of your skin
Hurts me—
Then I fall down again in a crook of your body
And the smoothness to come makes my fingers shake—
It's satin
You're glowing
Like a golden shell in the sunlight
Then it's not only poetry that covers your back
It's all the music in the world.

When I think of you it's like—

An explosion

Of little fragments of you

In me.

You're like a sunflower

Illuminating

All my insides.

*

I would kiss
All your traumas—
All your pains—
And all your tears.

Let me hold
All your secrets—
All your past—
Your memories.

Let me kiss
All your beauty—
All your gold—
And miseries.

There is a gold
That Men haven't sought—
It's the colour
Of your soul—
The colour—I picture you in—
The one—magnifying your limbs—

And all this gold
Is like a halo—
Runs like a veil
When you go—
The long veil—I can see you in—
The one—beautifying your skin—

She has the voice
That drills the air
That gives a rhythm to the pulse of the wind—
And that echoes the pulse of my heart—
She is the shadow—
The element of energy—
That feels like an extension of me—
Like—electricity—
She is the physicality of my personality
The expression of my being

                    She is the savage—unexpected—wave
                        Coming and drowning me
                    She is the flag flying in the air
                        Coming—going—
        She shows the direction of where Life must be—

A distant lighthouse
With eyes like honey
Which guide the movements of my hips
And all around—an ocean
Sometimes wild sometimes quiet
And all around—isolation
A rain of solitude—over me—

Obsession—is my name
I'm an endless pit of repeated questions
A self-feeding interest
An immortal crisis—a mental sickness

And I have the face of
Beauty—wearing a cream, caramel-like coat
And every step I make
Is singing—it's a melancholy echoing
Into the poet's ribs.

She is a sun
And with her rays she ignites
And fills in all the holes of emptiness.

Wanting to cure myself with a pen
I used it as a needle—and
Injected—in my heart and brain
The poison of love—

I am in love with Life—
With its whirlings, its screamings
O v e r w h e l m i n g sights
With its colours and energy—
I'm in love with its—
Unexpected laughs
And everywhere's presence
With its ups and downs
With its—
Uncontrollability
And passionate surprises—
Life has her face—
I am in love with Life—

Next time you enter my space—my world—
I'll breathe in your scent
Let it invade my throat, brain and chest
So as to not forget
What you smell like—when I'm alone
Like smoking-addicted folks' steal
Their neighbour's cloud of breath—

The waiting and receiving:

A veil
A curtain
Slowly falling down before me
A pause button pressed
Switching off the light of the world
Switching off the light in me—

Then a ghost
An elf
Or maybe she
Turns the light back on—

Like the Eiffel Tower
The Statue of Liberty—
I'm lit up again: I can see—
My eyes are open
The world—colourful, alive—
In motion again—
And I walk in it—

I want
You—

To be with you
A touch from you
Eye contact—

To sleep with you
A smile from you
Your back—

Your eyes
Your lips
Your nose
Your chin—
Your hands
Your arms
Your fingers
And skin—

It seems that—
When a weight grows in my stomach
—like the seed of a bad weed—
When all the faces I see are dark to me
—like a mourning veil on each of their smiles—
When I forget to breathe and what
Smiling feels like—
Well, it seems that—

Only you carry the answer
And you give it to me with this
Glowing smile of yours—
And finally, I can rest
With my heavy head—on your shoulder.

There is kindness everywhere
And she accepts all its little gifts
—like offerings she'd take for granted—
Never betrays—awkwardness—
It's simple—and easy—
To say yes—

She sees her own kindness
In all of us
And *this* is her Great Beauty.

I promise:
My eyes will be
A thick, brown blanket
Warming you
When you get cold—

—natural—

                    Our story
                Is the repetition
                    Of a story
                 We forgot about
                       And
                   Have lived
                   Already.

That's why it feels
So smooth
To be with you—
That's why it felt
So easy
To fall for you
And
Become your friend—

That's why everything feels like
                Honey
Running smoothly
Down our skins—

They can sense the change
Perhaps in the air I walk in
Or in the rebirth of my skin
I cannot tell—

They can't put their finger on
What took me away
Why I can't go back to their world—

It's just that I've been touched by
Gold—

A world of stares is before us
A world of blinks—

But they don't see the bridge
That I see
The bridge from which
On each extremity
We hold the tick-tock of time in our hands
Staring
At each other—
They don't see the tunnel
In which our voices echo—
They don't hear our heartbeats
Their equal pace—their resonance—
And they don't see
That your body
Is the limb I've lost on the way
That when it crawls onto mine—
Order—
And come what may—

Underneath the layers
Of what other people see—
Education
Self-discipline
Disillusion
Regrets, sorrow and self-understanding—

Our hearts are sisters
And beat equally
The tender hastened shaken
Bliss of agony—
We're twins who didn't grow
In the same womb—
But all my skin says so:
We're twins in harmony.

Your past and mine were braided
In *one same plait*
By an invisible hand—two decades ago—

It isn't Fate—it's a Common Ground.

A sensation of revolution
Of defiance
Of high chins and rebellion—
But—above all—
The certitude—soothing, exhilarating—
Of standing—or lying—
AS EQUALS
An addiction—
The rest—can no longer be seen—
It's like—meeting—a distant relative.

I am a woman
who loves
another woman
who loves
a woman
and that
one woman
is the woman
I am.

I'm
In need
Of the things
She wants
To tell me.

And I'll
Explode
With the things
I want
To tell her.

Want
Is a curious thing—
An open mind
Closed on one life
A missing piece
A perforated heart
A sick belly
A mutilated
Body
And a complete loss
Of lucidity
An obsession
A painful
D   E   L   I   R   I   U   M
A crude tension
Uncontrollable
Insanity—WANT
Is in all my body
It's all in me
I want—
I want—
I want—

Like a blade entering the wood
In ancient Japanese art
With rigour and concentration
Missing nothing of it
My hand will follow the lines of your back—

They are like—
       Traces
Of actions from the past
Of secrets to sort out
The scars on your face

My heart bleeds
For every drop of blood, you gave
To the tracing of your marks—
And I lick
All those tiny roads that look like veins
And your tears—and your taste—

My fingers run

Up and down your back

Rich in your beauty –

It's a matter of shoulder blades
Of neck skin really—

Choir:
My sex
My heart
My stomach
Sing the same tune
Together—

A touch:

A burning
A swelling
A dripping—

This is what
Your hand in my hair
Does to the middle of
My body.

—EUPHORIA

The captain
   Of the dancing waves—

                              The conductor
                        Of my singing emotions—

Exhaustion
From sleepless hours
From fluids flooding the nights—

Restlessness
Agony
When you French-kiss my beating core
The inside of me
My femininity—

                                        How
                                  Beautiful
                                  You are—

How
Hungry
I am
For you—

Love—
You don't have to do all the work
I want us to share—

If I get down on my knees
To touch your *salty* rink deep
I'll stream
Sense the shower coming—rolling—
In me—

The same way I'll feel
Your *slippery* ice
Turn
Into a *lake*—

But I'll wait for your flow
Take your pulse
Count your breaths
To melt—

In the end we won't know
Who spilled more water in
The bed—

Oh—it is a trembling body I have
Shaking hands
    And shaking legs
  PAINFUL OVARIES
      And a SCREAM from the skin
Coming alive
      A skin screaming
Separating from my flesh
  To cover your entire being—

What a perfect circle—
To breathe inside your skin—all night
To write about our night—all day

Have you seen on TV—
The thought you could get hurt
The possibility
The image of a gun
Of a finger
Pulling the trigger—
I go insane as I imagine
The sound of your voice calling for help
The despair in your heart
The panic—the tears
The incredible belief
That somebody out there
Might want to crush your lungs
To steal the air, I love to hear you breathe
Because your skin
I would have kissed and adored
The night before
Would be too glowing
Would blind them
And their absurdity
And because your golden beauty
Your hazel—your honey
Would be too much to bear
In a different way than for me—

She said—
Let
her
keep a trace of me
inside her

Let her ripen me
in her

Her body
would
remember—

It would
remember
the trace
I'd have
left—

I'm the rock
The piece that'll never move
The brick
The marble
My roots are sealed—

You're the wind
The veil flying
Dancing
The breath
Above me—

I'd rather be
ANGRY
At her:
There are
PRIDE
And DIGNITY
In ANGER—

But no strength
No reward
In being
Depressed
Because of someone else.

Pride was given—
Do I need to beg?
My heart sinks—falls down into the deepest
Tombs
My brain—my brain is lost—
Like a forgotten locket—
And you thief—run between the graves
Of Vision—Serenity—Reason
With a grin—on your HAUNTING face—

Am I a bird with which you play?
Do you feel proud of the control
You have on me?
This delicious pain in the clay
Of my bleeding, beating heart
On which you trace your indelible
Mark—

My heart
Didn't break exactly—
It became a *stone*
And that stone
Rolled
All the way down
To my stomach—
I felt
Extremely tired—suddenly—
For all the life
And all the youth in me
Had gone—

I thought of leaving
But I had no
Body.

187

I missed your touch—yesterday
And I couldn't sleep last night
I wanted to cry—for a day
But I almost lost sight
Of myself—

Now I'm drowning—again
In the memory of your eyes
Of when you looked away and didn't seem
To miss my burning eyes—

I wish
My mind could be read—or
Thoughts could be
Clouds with
Words in them
That would go from
One person to another like
Text messages—
Because I begged her to come to me
When she turned to me that last time—

But she is not
A mind reader
And thoughts are not clouds with
Words in them—

And so, she didn't come.

The water you're supposed to call

Sing for

And make flow down—

Instead soaked my eyes last night—

It needed to get out—somehow—

It's when night and silence slither in
That the weight of missing you creeps in
Like a bomb ticking
Counting
The seconds before exploding—

It's when peaceful quiet lures
That your voice in my head roars
And I'm left in here sinking—

How much the world changes in a few hours—
Noise—colours—physicality are gone—
The world now—
Is made of—
Stone—and ink.

If only I had magic fingers
To draw her silhouette in the distance—
Her silhouette—
Walking towards me—

The heart is suicidal—
How it craves to be broken
Throwing itself on the arrow
On the lethal thorn—

When I wander about your house
Like a starved stray dog
It's a call of love.
It happens when I can't help it:
When I miss you so much
It feels like
A weight of tears—in my womb—
When I need to get a touch of
Your world—what you know—
And even when you're away seeing your house
Helps me catch my breath—
And if I'm lucky I get to see
One of your relatives
And so, I search for every possible trace
Of you in them—

Then I go home
Relieved—

I'll track you
Investigate
Stop every white car on the road
Look for your face in the mobs
Interrupt people who look like you
Ask everyone you know about you

So, when I come across you
On the bus
In the street
It'll feel
Like a present from
Myself to myself
Like merit—

My legs have walked two hundred miles
My skin has dropped ten pounds of sweat
For since you went out of my sight
I need to make my flesh forget—

My arms, my sex, my chest and brain
Have carried you like extra weight
Have longed to pour you just like rain
And erase your departure date.

This time—
I choose me
Farewell—to your golden, heart-slashing claws
To the doubts of lead, you dropped in my head
Breaking in
On a January afternoon—
Farewell—to the honey almonds of your face
That intoxicate my common sense—
To your deafening voice that echoes in my brain—
and in all my veins—
This time—farewell

I thought you were a Sun—

But you're barely a torch
With no batteries.

The sun makes flowers bloom.
And you were the sun
And my heart the flower.

                              But you turned into a ball of ice
                                 And the air you blew
                                            Froze me
                                         To the root.

Can't believe my hands are still shaking
My insides
Still aching.

Roller coasters:

You're like the wind—
and can't be trusted.

I promised I had sworn—
To myself—at least ten
Determined—painful—times—
I promised—
I convinced myself—
I thought—
It was time to let her GO
To turn my eyes to some other wind
To let her—and all the whirl she dropped on her
way—
Fly back
To the mysterious world they came from!

But don't judge me, world—mirror—
Her air—keeps coming BACK
It is her golden veil—that only I can see—

And I—

Fall—fall

A little farther down—

She is the blow
　—and the cure

Missing you gets physical
You've become acid in my veins.

Hope is for the fools
But it's resilient—

It's a spark in the veins
A star in the heart
A refusal to submit
An agitator—an impatience—
It's survival.

Hope is Optimism
And even you couldn't kill mine
Cause I still turn around
When I hear a sound
That stands no chance to be yours—

And I wait all day long
For the Promised Hour—that never comes—

Hope is for the fools who still believe in magic
But it is resilient—

                    I put on a pretty dress
                       Some mascara on
        My summer tan is a silent invitation that I'm
                       sending you—

But staring at the gate
Waiting on the threshold
For news from you
Or for a sudden irruption of you
I feel like a war fiancée—

I keep staring—staring—
But the sun goes down
The walkers get few
Freshness has replaced the summer heat
I should fetch a jacket inside
But I fear to—
Then I'm being called for dinner
And still—nothing—

The night will be a stone in my belly
I'll be left imagining you

                       Until I wake up
                       Put on a pretty dress
                         Some mascara on
                         Stare at the gate
                    And wait on the threshold
                             For you.

It's a story of ups and downs—
Of hope and despair—
And of something in between.

A doubt
entering my troubled mind—

Have I dreamed her

    all this time?

My hope is
like a phoenix—

It's an immortal
long-clawed creature

Digging into
my flesh

Searching for a next illusion
to grasp—
and never let go.

It's a
never-ending
process

Of climbing
up
and falling
down

Like a lift
teased
by young children.

Never-lasting joys are not to be looked down
For even when missing you eats my heart alive
There're still—
The promise of a blue sky
A four-year-old cousin's smile
A barbecue organized next week
The *Harry Potter* saga on the telly

An inside joke between sisters
A novel on the bedside table

The certainty of thousands of future
Never-lasting joys

And the never-dying—sleeping—hope
To heal soon—

I thought that it was you—

But it was me—
It was me all along—

It was me here
In here—
It was *I*
Who was being strong—

A layer of wounded love
Can only be covered
By another layer of love—

In the end we're all
Wrapped-up bodies.

She was my lighthouse
She was my dock
When I was lost at sea—

She was my lighthouse
She was my dock
When I was lost at sea—

I'm there—
I'll always be there—
Where everything is yours
Where it has all started
Where you are everywhere
Where even the trees have your scent—
I'll always be there.

You laid your palm flat on my heart
Leaving a mark
Then you disappeared—